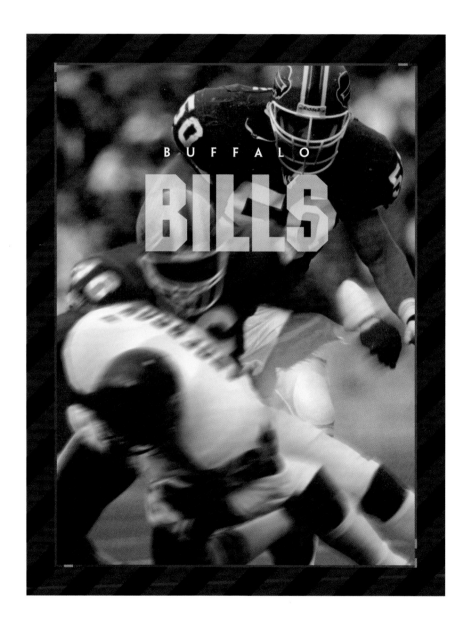

BUFFALO

BILLS

LOREN STANLEY

CREATIVE ⬤ EDUCATION

Published by Creative Education
123 South Broad Street, Mankato, Minnesota 56001
Creative Education is an imprint of The Creative Company

Designed by Rita Marshall
Cover illustration by Rob Day

Photos by: Allsport Photography, Associated Press, Bettmann Archive,
Duomo, Focus on Sports, Fotosport, and SportsChrome.

Library of Congress Cataloging-in-Publication Data

Stanley, Loren 1951-
Buffalo Bills / by Loren Stanley.
p. cm. — (NFL Today)
Summary: Traces the history of the team from its beginnings through 1996.
ISBN 0-88682-791-4

1. Buffalo Bills (Football team)—History—Juvenile literature.
[1. Buffalo Bills (Football team) 2. Football—History.]
I. Title. II. Series.

GV956. B83S83 1996   96-15231
796.332'64'0974797—dc20

123456

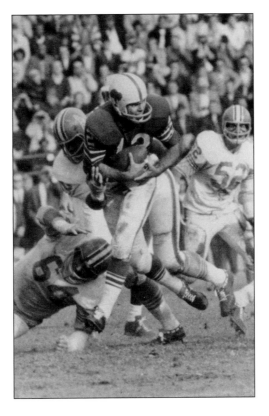

Like so many cities along the Great Lakes, Buffalo, New York is held captive every winter by huge snowfalls. The people who live in this northern city look for winter activities each year to capture their interest and fill their weekends with fun. Watching sports, especially football, is one way to survive the long, cold, snowy winters. But residents of Buffalo have not always had the chance to see professional football in their city.

When the All-America Football Conference merged with the National Football League in 1950, Buffalo lost its beloved team, becoming one of the many major American cities without a

A Bills star from the past, Daryle Lamonica (#12).

Fullback Cookie Gilchrist established a new AFL season rushing record with 1,096 yards.

pro football club. A city that thrived on sports, Buffalo was eager to attract another franchise. The National Football League, however, was not about to grant Buffalo its wish.

Enter Lamar Hunt, the man Americans sometimes describe as the "Catsup King." Hunt, a wealthy Texas businessman who made his fortune selling Hunt's Catsup, petitioned the NFL to let him start a new football team. When the league refused, Hunt contacted seven interested friends. This "Foolish Club," as the group of eight risktakers came to be known, formed a new football league, the American Football League (AFL).

One of Hunt's partners was Ralph C. Wilson, an avid football fan. When Lamar Hunt suggested reviving football in Buffalo, Wilson contacted city leaders and signed a lease on the city's War Memorial Stadium in November 1959. Today, over 35 years later, Wilson and his family still manage the franchise. He has been the club's only president and is the man responsible for returning football to Buffalo.

A TEAM AT LAST

The team did not have a winning season in 1960 or 1961, but not for a lack of fan enthusiasm. Named the Bills after Buffalo's earlier team, which had been given its name in honor of Western hero Buffalo Bill Cody, the club got an unexpected "welcome home" parade on July 29, 1960. The day before its exhibition game, over 100,000 cheering fans crowded Buffalo streets to welcome their new team to the city.

The Bills' rebirth as an AFL team was directed first by Garrard "Buster" Ramsey, a former guard and defensive coach for the Detroit Lions, and later by Lou Saban, the former Boston Patriots

Bruce Smith led the Bills defense in the 1990s (page 7).

1 9 6 4

Buffalo captured the AFL championship with a 20-7 triumph over San Diego.

coach. A man with a hot temper, Ramsey lasted only two years as Buffalo's head man. He once threatened to throw a player out the window of an airplane for performing badly on the field.

Lou Saban, who coached Buffalo from 1962 to 1965 and again from 1972 to 1976, proved more popular. Saban, who led the Bills to AFL championships in 1964 and 1965, had been a quarterback at Indiana University in the early 1940s. After serving in World War II, he became a linebacker with the All-American Football Conference's Cleveland Browns. Between 1946 and 1949, he played many games against the original Bills. After retiring as a player, Saban began a college coaching career in 1950. Twelve years later, he brought lots of needed experience to the young Bills.

As the Bills' head coach, Saban had an amazing ability to choose players with hidden potential and turn them into winners on the field. Among those early stars were wide receiver Elbert Dubenion, fullback Cookie Gilchrist, kicker Pete Gogolak, and quarterbacks Jack Kemp and Daryle Lamonica.

Elbert Dubenion, from small Bluffton College, became the Bills' first star. His ability to read defenses, snatch passes out of the air under pressure, and run for additional yardage earned him the nickname "Golden Wheels." It also earned him Bills pass reception records that still stand today.

Cookie Gilchrist came to Buffalo in 1962 from the Canadian Football League and immediately proved his value as a fullback. The first AFL back to gain over 1,000 yards in a season, Gilchrist, at 6-foot-3 and 251 pounds, was nearly impossible to bring down as he bulled toward the goal posts. In one stunning performance against the New York Jets, Gilchrist ran for five touchdowns and 243 yards, helping Buffalo rout New York 45-14.

Pete Gogolak, signed in 1964 from Cornell University, brought a new style of kicking to the AFL. Gogolak kicked the football using a soccer-style kick. At first, the fans thought he looked funny, but his strange method was effective—Gogolak scored 47 field goals in his two years with the team.

The signal-calling duo of Jack Kemp and Daryle Lamonica led the Bills to five consecutive winning seasons (1962-1966). Instead of displaying the usual rivalry between quarterbacks jockeying for the top position, Kemp, the starter, and Lamonica, the reliever, worked smoothly, like a well-oiled machine, to create one of the league's most dangerous offensive teams.

Kemp, a 1957 graduate of Occidental College, came to Buffalo in mid-1962 from the San Diego Chargers. Although he only appeared in four games that year with his new team, he ended up in the AFL All-Star game and produced a winning season for a team that had begun the year with five straight losses. Kemp played in Buffalo until 1969, when he retired from football. Since his playing days, he has served in the U.S. House of Representatives and as President George Bush's Secretary of Housing and Urban Development. The AFL's Most Valuable Player in 1965 now enjoys a prestigious career in our nation's capital.

In 1967, Coach Saban's departure to the University of Maryland and trades that took Daryle Lamonica and Cookie Gilchrist weakened the championship team. It was the end of an era, but what an era it had been. Seven-year-old Buffalo already claimed five winning seasons and two AFL championships.

1 9 6 7

Can-do Kemp! Quarterback Jack Kemp passed for 2,500 yards and fourteen touchdowns.

The Bills offense digs in (pages 10-11).

Bills quarterback Jack Kemp provided veteran leadership and passed for 2,503 yards.

Two dismal seasons in 1967 and 1968 took the Bills to the basement of the AFL standings. The only thing to look forward to was the number one draft pick given to Buffalo in the spring 1969 draft. It was the team's reward for finishing so low in the standings. Little did Buffalo fans or players know that their draftee, Heisman Trophy winner O.J. Simpson, would become one of football's greatest stars.

Orenthal James Simpson, known during his playing days as "O.J." or simply "The Juice," was the object of every coach's interest when he finished school at the University of Southern California in May 1969. While a senior, he had broken NCAA records for carries and rushing yards. When balloting was completed for the Heisman in 1968, Simpson won by the largest point margin ever.

In addition to playing football at Southern Cal., Simpson was also part of the world record-setting USC 440-yard relay team. Because of this accomplishment he was often called "the fastest man in cleats."

While O.J. Simpson was definitely a welcome sight in Buffalo, he called his early years in a Bills' uniform the "three lost years." He felt this way because of Buffalo coach John Rauch's idea about Simpson's love for running the ball. "That's not my style," Rauch argued. "I couldn't build my offense around one back, no matter how good he is." Meanwhile, Simpson felt his skills were getting rusty. He ran for less than 700 hundred yards in 1969 and 1970, rarely scored, and saw his team endure three more demoralizing seasons. Simpson pondered quitting the team until Rauch picked a quarrel with owner Ralph Wilson and soon thereafter left the squad. The Bills endured one more losing season before Lou Saban, Buffalo's miracle worker, returned to coach the Bills in 1972.

Saban's arrival encouraged Simpson and his teammates. They knew Saban was tough and demanding, but they also liked the idea that the coach favored the running game and was honest about what he expected from his players. As he told the team after handing Simpson the ball, "There's your meal ticket. Block for him." And block they did. With 1,251 yards, Simpson won the league rushing title in 1972. Even though the team only finished with a 4-9-1 season, morale was definitely on the upswing.

Much of this change in attitude can be traced to coach Saban's creation of "the Electric Company," an offensive unit designed to turn on "the Juice." Through trades, waivers and the college draft, Saban gathered an impressive cast of characters. The draft brought players like Joe DeLamielleure, Reggie McKenzie and Joe Ferguson, while other maneuvers brought Dave Foley, Mike Montler, Jeff Winans and J.D. Hill to help fill out the roster.

The Electric Company demonstrated its awesome prowess in the December 16, 1973 matchup at home with the New York Jets. On the cold playing field that day, O.J. Simpson and his teammates scored one for the record books.

Before this game, the offensive line had already given Buffalo its first winning season in six years. It had also, in thirteen games, given Simpson 1,803 yards rushing, only sixty yards short of Jim Brown's longstanding season rushing record. This was the last game of the regular season. In the icy cold that froze both hands and feet, Simpson's blockers punched holes in the Jets'

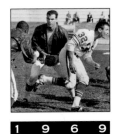

The Bills gathered at East Aurora, New York, for the club's first training camp.

O.J. Simpson rushed for 2,003 yards and averaged 6.0 yards per carry.

defense. By the fourth quarter, O.J. Simpson, to the cheers of the fans, had broken Brown's record. He had gained 2,003 yards in one season, a record that stood until 1984. Play stopped, players from both teams congratulated him, the fans roared, and Simpson's proud teammates carried him off the field.

The Juice and his offensive line ran the Bills to two more victorious seasons in 1974 and 1975, and Simpson's impressive list of records grew even longer. But Simpson was unhappy. The 1976 season ended with a frustrating 2-12 record for the Bills. Lou Saban's resignation and the departure by trade of such talents as Ahmad Rashad, Pat Toomay, J.D. Hill, and other team members weakened the Bills. Finally, an October 30, 1977 game against Seattle left Simpson with a reinjured knee. He asked to be traded. He wanted to go home, and he wanted his chance to play in a Super Bowl. He got his wish in March 1978 when the Bills' new coach, former Los Angeles Rams skipper Chuck Knox, traded Simpson to the San Francisco 49ers for five future draft choices.

While it took him two years to rebuild his new team, Chuck Knox used his time and his five draft picks wisely to create a strong defensive. Knox already had a strong offense. Joe Ferguson had blossomed under O.J. Simpson's tutelage.

Some people felt Ferguson had football in his blood. A Louisiana native, he joined fellow Louisianans Terry Bradshaw, Bert Jones, and Doug Williams in the ranks of those few men who get to quarterback pro teams. His Woodland High School coach, who had also coached Bradshaw, compared Ferguson to the great Pittsburgh Steelers quarterback. Similar praise was heaped on him by Frank Broyles, coach of his college team, the University of Arkansas Razorbacks.

While at Arkansas, Ferguson perfected the long-bomb

O.J. Simpson became a star in the 1970s.

*Rookie nose tackle
Fred Smerlas began
a Bills career that
would last a decade.*

passes that made him the Bills' leading passer from 1973 to 1984. Voted an All-American during his junior year, Ferguson was drafted by the Bills in 1973, arriving just as O.J. Simpson's greatest season began. The two became friends, and the great runner taught the young quarterback a few tricks of the game.

The other mainstay of the Buffalo offense was a young running back who came to the Bills as part of the O.J. Simpson trade. A second-round draft pick, Auburn's Joe Cribbs was a good investment. As teammate Mario Clark said, "I like to call him Joe 'Houdini' Cribbs, as in escape artist. Even when you get him in your hands, you can't tackle him. He just sort of squirts through your fingers." Cribbs led Buffalo in rushing for four straight seasons, and only O.J. Simpson ranks ahead of Cribbs in total yards rushed in a Buffalo uniform.

While the offense carried much of the load, Knox carefully built a solid defense to eventually support them. With high draft picks coach Knox selected Fred Smerlas and Jim Haslett, standouts at Boston College and Indiana University of Pennsylvania. Isiah Robertson and Phil Villipiano, both linebackers, were obtained in trades with the Los Angeles Rams and the Oakland Raiders.

Knox led the Bills to playoff appearances in 1980 and 1981. Although they didn't make it as far as the Super Bowl in either year, their last-second pass interception and ensuing 31-27 victory over the New York Jets in the 1981 playoffs convinced skeptics that the Bills were now strong contenders. The glory years seemed to be back.

A 57-day players' strike and resulting short season in 1982 upset Coach Knox's carefully laid rebuilding plans. The loss of such stars as Joe Cribbs over salary disputes further tarnished

Quarterback Joe Ferguson was a touchdown leader in the 1980s.

the winners. Discouraged, Knox himself left for a new job in Seattle in 1982.

1 9 8 2

Speedy and power-ful running back Joe Cribbs averaged 4.7 yards per carry.

Knox's trusted assistant Kay Stephenson took over the head coaching duties. Although Stephenson was able to coach his injury-ridden team to an 8-8 record in 1983, neither he, nor his successor Hank Bullough, were able to sustain the ailing Bills. The club's record sank to 2-14 in 1984 and 1985 and 4-12 in 1986. Individual standouts such as running back Greg Bell, punter John Kidd, and quarterback Joe Dufek turned in fine performances, but the team didn't rise from the division cellar.

The turnaround would be led by Marv Levy, named Bills head coach in 1986. Levy brought extensive experience to his new post. After coaching future Dallas Cowboy star Craig Morton at the University of California and serving as head coach at the College of William and Mary, Levy assisted Jerry Williams in

Philadelphia and George Allen in Los Angeles and Washington. His head coaching career included a stint with the Kansas City Chiefs.

Levy was able to quickly redirect the Bills' course. In 1987 he led them to a 7-8 record and in 1988 and 1989 he brought them to the top of the AFC's Eastern Division.

INTO THE 1990s

Head coach Marv Levy acheived the first of many playoff appearances with the Bills.

Levy was blessed with an impressive list of young players to develop. Defensive end Bruce Smith, an All-American at Virginia Tech, was among the league's most feared pass rushers. He and linebacker Cornelius Bennett were among those to become perennial Pro Bowlers. Free safety Mark Kelso, a free agent who signed with Buffalo in 1986, had some of the nimblest fingers in the AFC. He was valued for his ability to intercept passes and run them in to score. Like many pro players, Mark was active in local charities—something that often doesn't get into the news. He raised $4,200 in 1988 by pledging money for each interception, fumble recovery, and tackle he made during the season.

Leading the offense was Buffalo's star quarterback, Jim Kelly, called "our future" by former coach Hank Bullough. Kelly came to the Bills in 1986 after two seasons with the USFL's Houston Gamblers. One of five brothers who played collegiate football, Kelly quarterbacked the University of Miami Hurricanes to a Peach Bowl appearance in 1980. A popular figure in Buffalo, Kelly had his own radio and television shows. Like Kelso, he was also active in charity work and has raised over $1,000,000 to help Buffalo-area children.

On the football field he was equally successful. In 1989, the

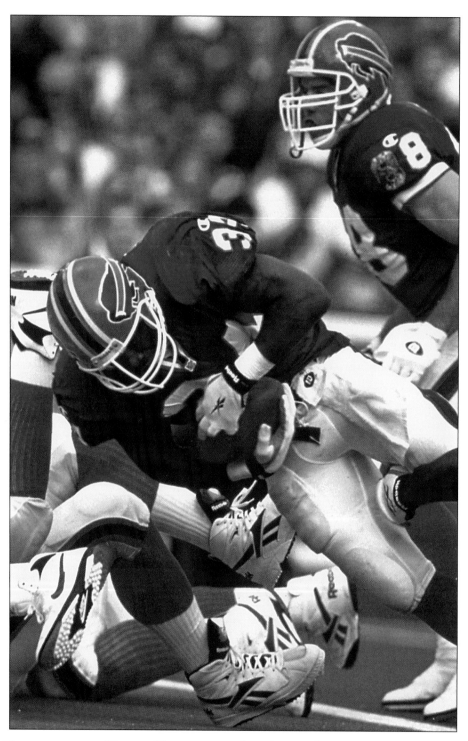

Thurman Thomas was a rushing threat in the 1990s.

Bills were the NFL's second-highest scoring team, trailing only the Super Bowl bound San Francisco 49ers. Much of this was due to Kelly's strong arm. The following year, Kelly achieved one of the highest quarterback ratings (101.3) in NFL history and was selected to the Pro Bowl.

But Kelly was not the only star. Two young players had emerged alongside him to share the spotlight—and to form the nucleus of the greatest offensive unit in Bills history.

The first was wide receiver Andre Reed, an unheralded fourth-round draft pick by the Bills in 1985. Reed played his college ball at Kutztown University in Pennsylvania—hardly a hotbed for emerging pro football talent. But Reed soon established himself as Kelly's favorite long-range target and as a perennial choice for the Pro Bowl. Reed has gone on to break virtually every Bills receiving record and ranks as the fifth-leading all-time pass catcher in NFL history.

The second was running back Thurman Thomas, a second-round choice from Oklahoma State in 1988. Thomas, at 5-foot-10 and 198 pounds, was relatively small by NFL standards. But that didn't stop him from becoming one of the most versatile—and feared—backfield talents of his era. Adept both as a runner and as a receiver, Thomas set a new NFL record by leading the league in total yardage for four consecutive years—from 1989 to 1992. Like Reed and Kelly, Thomas made frequent appearances in the Pro Bowl.

Wide receiver Andre Reed caught 81 passes for 1,113 yards and 10 touchdowns.

Left to right: Bruce Smith, Jim Kelly, Thurman Thomas, Cornelius Bennett.

With a defense led by Smith and Bennett and an offensive starring Kelly, Reed and Thomas, the Bills possessed remarkable talent. But what Buffalo accomplished in the first four years of the 1990s was more than remarkable—it was unparalleled in NFL history.

Quarterback Jim Kelly passed for over 3,500 yards in his first season with the Bills.

The Bills appeared in four straight Super Bowls. None of the dominant teams of the past can make such a claim.

True, the Bills lost all four of those Super Bowls. But that does not diminish the team effort and dedication that went into achieving such a consistently high standard of excellence. Buffalo lost in its first Super Bowl appearance by the narrowest of margins—by one point to the New York Giants. That Super Bowl, played on January 27, 1991, has been called "A Game for the Ages."

In the first half, the two powerhouse teams showed just how evenly matched they were. The Giants began the scoring with a field goal, which was matched by a 23-yard field goal by Buffalo kicker Scott Norwood. Then, in the second quarter, the Bills scored a touchdown on a 1-yard plunge by running back Don Smith. This was followed by a Super Bowl rarity—a safety scored when Buffalo defensive end Bruce Smith tackled Giants quarterback Jeff Hostetler in the end zone. But the Giants countered with an 87-yard scoring drive. Still, Buffalo went into the locker room at halftime with a 12-10 lead.

The Giants opened the second half with another long scoring drive to forge in front 17-12. But in the fourth quarter, Thurman Thomas scampered 31 yards for a touchdown that regained the lead for Buffalo 19-17. The Giants came back once

Thurman Thomas was a dominant running back in the 1990s (pages 26-27).

Veteran All-Pro linebacker Chris Spielman spearheads the Bills defense with his aggressive play.

more, kicking a field goal to go ahead 20-19 and place the pressure squarely on the Bills, who launched their final offensive drive from their own 10-yard line with just over two minutes left in the game. They marched 61 yards and then, with four seconds remaining, Norwood lined up for a 47-yard field goal attempt. This time, however, he missed—the ball sailed just right of the goal post as the game clock ran out.

As one sportswriter put it, "That is the way that all Super Bowls ought to be played."

Unfortunately, Buffalo did not fare as well in the next three Super Bowls, losing to the Washington Redskins 37-24 and then twice in succession to the Dallas Cowboys by wide margins— 52-17 and 30-13. But those scores do not tell the whole story. The Bills had to overcome stiff competition each year just to return to the Super Bowl.

During the 1992 playoffs, for example, Buffalo came back from a 35-3 deficit to beat the Houston Oilers 41-38. And they did so despite the fact that Jim Kelly was injured and unavailable for the game. Reserve quarterback Frank Reich led a heroic effort that included four Bills touchdowns in under seven minutes in the third quarter. When Buffalo kicker Steve Christie booted the winning 32-yard field goal in sudden-death overtime, it marked the greatest point-margin comeback in NFL history.

But the Bills do not intend to rest on their laurels. In 1995 they rebounded from an off-year to regain their familiar position as champions of the AFC Eastern Division. A new Buffalo defensive star emerged during the season—linebacker Bryce Paup, who teamed with Smith to form a devastating sack threat to opposing quarterbacks. (One admiring sportswriter dubbed

Defensive end Bruce Smith was a mighty force in the 1990s.

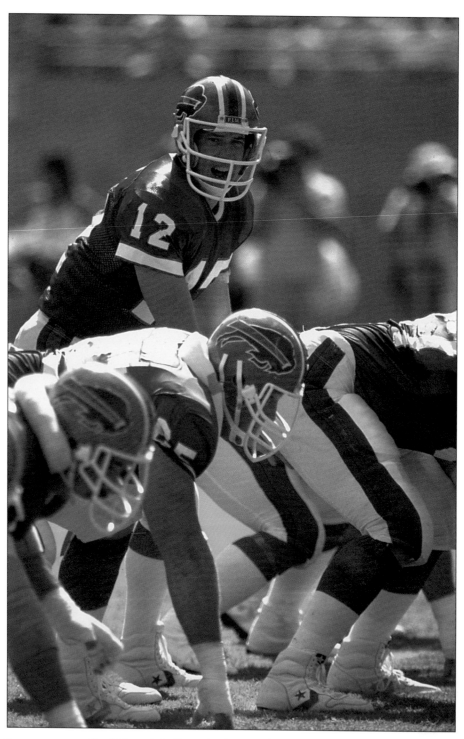

Jim Kelly posted all-time leading marks in passing yardage.

Linebacker Bryce Paup specialized in sacking opposing quarterbacks.   31

Paup "King Kong" and Smith "Godzilla.") The Bills went on to post an impressive 37-22 first-round playoff win over the Miami Dolphins before losing to the Pittsburgh Steelers.

The Bills' tradition of excellence is alive and well. Both the team and its loyal Buffalo fans retain the ultimate dream of winning the Super Bowl. After the heights they have enjoyed, nothing less will satisfy them. That is the challenge that will motivate them through the 1990s.